GIGGLE TILL YOU JIGGLE

Silly Jokes, Riddles and Tongue Twisters for Kids

Cillian Bookless

BOOK PEOPLE PRESS

Disclaimer Notice:
The information contained in this book is for educational and entertainment purposes only. The content in this book has been derived from various sources as well as original material. Under no circumstances is the author responsible for any losses, direct or indirect, that are incurred as a result of the use of information contained within this book, including but not limited to errors, inaccuracies and omissions.

ISBN-13: 978139999005

ISBN-10: 1399990055

Cover design by: E.M. Bookless

Contents

Animal Jokes.. 4

Food Jokes..21

Eww!! Gross Jokes 31

Super Silly Side-Splitters.................................36

Spooky Jokes 43

Things That Go Jokes 51

Rib-Tickling Random Jokes..............................57

Knock Knock Jokes 77

Ridiculous Riddles 89

Tongue Twisters 103

Animal Jokes

Why can't dinosaurs clap?

Because they are extinct.

What do cats have for breakfast?

Mice crispies.

Why don't crabs like to share?

Because they're shellfish!

What do dogs and trees have in common?

Bark!

Why does a giraffe have a long neck?

> **Because his feet stink!**

Why are gophers so good at golf?

> **Because when they see a yard, they make a hole in one!**

What's a cat's favorite color?

> **Purrrrrple!**

Where do chickens stay on vacation?

> **The Chick Inn!**

Where do you find a dog with no legs?

> **Right where you left him!**

Why don't koalas count as bears?

They don't have the koalafications.

Why can't leopards hide?

Because they are always spotted.

What do you give a dog with a fever?

Mustard, because it goes well with a hot dog.

What day of the week do chickens hide?

Fri-day.

Why did the chicken cross the playground?

To get to the other slide.

Why do seagulls fly over the sea?

Because if they flew over the bay, they would be bagels!

Why can't you trust the king of the jungle?

Because he is always lion.

Why do dogs love going to the Natural History Museum?

Because it's full of bones!

What do you call a pig that knows karate?

A pork chop.

Why do bees have sticky hair?

They use honeycombs.

What did the judge say when a skunk walked into the court?

Odor in the court!

What's more amazing than a talking rabbit?

A spelling bee!

What's the strongest animal?

A snail. It carries its house on its back!

What is the best way to catch a fish?

Have someone throw it to you.

What did the worm say to the other worm when he came home late?

Where on earth have you been?

How to fleas travel from place to place?

They itch-hike.

What do you call a parrot at the North Pole?

Lost.

Why can't dinosaurs sing?

Because they are extinct! Remember?

What do you call five giraffes?

A high five.

Which animal has the best writing?

A pen-guin.

Why don't lions eat clowns?

They taste funny.

What do you call a sheep with no legs?

A cloud.

Why are elephants big and grey?

Because if they were small and purple, they would be grapes!

What do you call a monkey that flies?

A hot air baboon.

What did the duck say to the cashier?

Put it on my bill.

What creature works for the CIA?

A spy-der.

Why can't bears operate the remote?

They keep pressing the paws button.

What type of bee can't make up its mind?

A maybe.

What do you get from an overly pampered cow?

Spoiled milk.

What kind of dinosaur loves to sleep?

A stega-snore-us.

What do you get when you cross a cow and a duck?

Cheese and quackers.

What did the leopard say after eating the antelope?

That hit the spot.

What do you call a bird on an airplane?

Lazy.

Why do they put bells on cows?

Because their horns don't work.

Why do dragons sleep during the day?

Because they fight knights.

How does a farmer count his cows?

With a cow-culator.

What do farmers say to cows that stay up late?

It's pasture bedtime.

What do you get when you cross an elephant with a fish?

Swimming trunks.

Why are frogs so happy?

They eat whatever bugs them.

What do you call a rabbit with fleas?

Bugs bunny.

When bulls shop, how do they pay?

They charge it.

What do porcupines say when they kiss?

Ouch!

Where do spiders get married?

At webbings.

Who is the angriest monkey?

Furious George.

Why are cats good at video games?

They have 9 lives.

Why do porcupines always win?

They have the most points.

What do you do if it rains cats and dogs?

You watch out for poodles.

Why are ducks the best detectives?

They always quack the case.

What do you call an alligator in a vest?

An investigator.

Which fish are at the bottom of the ocean?

The ones that dropped out of school.

Which key doesn't open a door or a lock?

A mon-key.

Why did the bird go to the hospital?

It needed tweetment.

Why did the boy put a cow on his trampoline?

He wanted a milkshake.

What do you get if you cross a cat with a lemon?

A sour puss.

What is it called when a cat wins at a dog show?

A cat-has-trophy.

Which dog keeps good time?

A watch dog.

What will make an octopus laugh?

Ten tickles.

What do cows like to watch?

Moovies.

What kind of egg does an evil chicken lay?

A devilled egg.

Why do birds fly south?

Because it's easier than walking there.

Which bird works at a construction site?

A crane.

How does a chicken stay in shape?

Eggs-ercise.

What is the loudest pet?

A trum-pet.

What do you call birds that stick together?

Vel-crows!

What do you get if you cross a kangaroo and a sheep?

A woolly jumper.

Why do cats make terrible storytellers?

Because they only have one tail.

What do you call a sleeping bull?

A bull-dozer!

What do you call a cow that likes honey?

Winnie-the-Moo!

How do you know which end of a worm is its head?

Tickle its middle and see which end giggles.

How do you know if there is an elephant under your bed?

Your nose touches the ceiling.

Food Jokes

Where does superman buy groceries?

In the supermarket.

What do you call a very big pumpkin?

A plumpkin!

What do you use to fix a broken pumpkin?

A pumpkin patch.

What do you call cheese that is not yours?

Nacho cheese.

What did one plate say to the other?

Dinner is on me.

How do you make an egg roll?

You push it.

What's the best thing to put into a pie?

Your teeth!

What did the egg say to her friend?

Have an egg-sellent day!

Why did the strawberry need help?

He was in a jam.

Where do hamburgers dance?

At the meat ball.

What did the hamburger name his daughter?

Patty.

Where do you learn to make banana splits?

At sundae school.

How can you tell if a clock is hungry?

It goes back four seconds.

Why did the banana go to the doctor?

It wasn't peeling well.

How many cherries grow on a cherry tree?

All of them.

What does the big tomato say when the little tomato walks too slow?

Ketchup!

What is a plumber's least favorite vegetable?

Leeks.

Yesterday a man threw a glass of milk on me!

How dairy!

What did the potato say just before getting skinned?

This does not a-peel to me!

What do you call two bananas?

A pair of slippers.

What tower eats a lot?

The I full tower.

Why did the baker stop making donuts?

He got sick of the hole thing!

Why did the scarecrow stop eating?

He was stuffed.

When do you spread peanut butter on the road?

When there is a traffic jam.

What fixes broken tomatoes?

Tomato paste.

What do eggs do in an emergency?

Scramble.

Why do reporters eat ice cream?

So they can get the scoop.

What did bacon say to tomato?

Lettuce get together.

What is pink, fuzzy and wears sunglasses?

A peach on vacation.

What can you eat when you're so hungry you need 2,000 of something?

Rice.

Why don't you starve in a desert?

Because of all the sand which is there.

Why did the mushroom go to all the parties?

He was a fun guy.

Why didn't the teddy bear order dessert?

Because it was stuffed.

What did the egg say to the clown?

You crack me up!

Why don't eggs tell jokes?

Because they'd crack each other up!

What sound does a nut make when it sneezes?

Cashew.

What do you get when you play Tug-of-War with a pig?

Pulled-Pork.

What is a ghost's favorite dessert?

Ice scream and boo-berries.

Waiter, waiter, will my pizza be long?

No sir, it will be round!

Did you hear about the boy who got hit in the head with a can of soda?

Luckily it was a soft drink.

What do you call a pizza with no toppings?

Mushroom for improvement.

What kind of vegetable is not welcome on a ship?
A leek.

What is a librarian's favorite vegetable?

Quiet peas!

Why do French people like to eat snails?

Because they are not fans of fast food.

What do you call a sad strawberry?

A blueberry.

Why did the melon jump into the pool?

Because it wanted to be a watermelon.

EWW!! Gross jokes

What do you call someone who wears a nappy to a party?

A party pooper!

What do you call superman after he's done a poo?

Pooperman.

What do you call a cave man's fart?

A blast from the past!

What does a panda say when he needs to go to the toilet?

Mr. Bamboo to the loo...!

What comes out of your nose at 150 mph?

A *Lambogreeny.*

What's another name for a snail?

A booger wearing a crash helmet.

What did one toilet say to the other?

You look flushed.

Why was the sand wet?

Because the sea weed.

Why can't you hear a pterodactyl go to the bathroom?

Because the pee is silent.

What's invisible and smells like worms?

A bird's fart.

Who are the most dangerous farters in the world?

Ninjas. They're silent but deadly.

What is a bathroom fairy called?

Stinkerbell.

Why do people fall asleep in the bathroom?

Because it's also called a restroom.

Why did the toilet roll down the hill?

To get to the bottom!

Why did three witches call in the plumber?

Hubble bubble, toilet trouble!

What is something you never appreciate until it's gone?

Toilet paper.

What do you get if you sit under a cow?

A pat on the head!

Super Silly Side-Splitters

Doctor! I only have 50 seconds to live!

Hang on, give me a minute.

What do you call a fish with no eyes?

A fsh.

What is a little bear with no teeth called?

A gummy bear.

What did the left eye say to the right eye?

Something between us smells.

Why is a rabbit like a plum?

> **They are both purple... except for the rabbit.**

What does everyone get for their birthday?

> **Older.**

What prize did the person who invented the knock knock joke win?

> **The no bell prize.**

What did the pig say on a hot day?

> **I'm bacon.**

What did the girl toss her alarm clock out the window?

> **To see time fly.**

What is red and bad for your teeth?

A brick.

How do you raise a baby elephant?

With a crane.

Why are French fries not really French?

They are cooked in Greece.

I wrote a song about a tortilla...

...actually, it's more of a wrap.

Why is *drool* such a great word?

It rolls off the tongue.

Where do you go if you get injured in a peek-a-boo accident?

The ICU.

What do you do if you're scared of elevators?

Take steps to avoid them.

What did Batman say to Robin just before they got in the Batmobile?

"Robin, get in the Batmobile."

I took the shell off my snail to make him faster, but it made him more **sluggish.**

Why are roof jokes free?

They are on the house.

Have you heard the joke about the jump rope?

Never mind, skip it.

What do Alexander the Great and Winnie the Pooh have in common?

They have the same middle name.

How do you stop your brother smelling?

Hold his nose.

What do you call someone with no body and no nose?

Nobody knows.

What is brown and sticky?

A stick.

Who is the king or queen of the pencil case?

The ruler.

Why did the melon jump into the pool?

Because it wanted to be a watermelon.

What do you call a monkey with bananas in both ears?

Anything you like, she can't hear you.

What wobbles around in a pram?

A jelly baby!

What do you call Batman and Robin after they were squashed by a road roller?

Flatman and Ribbon.

What did the grape say when he got stepped on?

Nothing, he just let out a little wine.

If you had one dollar, and then asked your dad for a dollar, how much money would you have?

One dollar.

What do you call a boomerang that doesn't come back?

A stick!

Spooky Jokes

What sort of jokes do skeletons like?

Bone ticklers.

What's the first thing a monster eats after getting his teeth checked?

The dentist.

Why didn't the skeleton go to the party?

He had no body to go with.

What room does a ghost not need in its house?

A living room.

What do ghosts do at sleepovers?

They tell scary human stories.

Why did the zombie stay home from school?

She felt rotten.

Why are vampires so unpopular?

Because they are pains in the neck!

What streets do zombies live on?

Dead ends.

Why don't skeletons take dangerous risks?

They don't have the guts.

What do ghosts eat to stay cool?

I-scream.

What does Dracula watch on TV?

Neck flix.

Why did the robot ghost haunt the graveyard?

Because it couldn't rust in peace.

Where do ghosts live?

They don't.

What do you do when 20 ghosts visit your house?

You hope it's Halloween!

Which song do vampires hate?

You Are My Sunshine.

How do ghosts like their eggs?

Terri-fried!

Did you hear about the giant monster who ate too many houses?

It was home sick.

Who cleans the haunted school?

The Scare-taker.

What did the skeleton say to the waiter?

Can I have an orange juice and a mop please?

How do you make a milkshake?

You tell it a scary story.

What do you call a witch that lives at the beach?

A sand witch!

What do ghosts use to wash their hair?

Sham-*boo.*

How can you tell if a vampire has a cold?

He starts coffin.

What do witches put on their bagels?

Scream cheese!

What happens when a ghost gets
in the fog?

He is mist!

What do you get when you cross a vampire and a
snowman?

Frostbite!

What type of pasta do ghosts like?

Spook-etti.

Where does Dracula keep his money?

In a blood bank!

Why are ghosts so bad at lying?

Because you can see right through them!

How do monsters like their coffee?

With scream and sugar.

Why couldn't Dracula's wife sleep?

Because of his coffin!

What is a vampire's favorite fruit?

A neck-tarine!

Patient: "Doctor, Doctor, I think I'm a vampire!

Doctor: "Necks, please!"

Things That Go Jokes

What did the traffic light say to the car?

Don't look, I'm about to change.

What only starts to work after it's fired?

A rocket!

Do you know the hardest thing about learning to ride a bike?

The road.

What happens when a frog's car breaks down?

It gets toad.

What did the cowboy say to the Audi?

Howdy Audi.

What do you call a Lamborghini Huracan that won't go?

A Hura-cant.

What has four wheels and flies?

A garbage truck.

What do you get when dinosaurs crash their cars?

Tyrannosaurus wrecks.

What has one horn and gives milk?

A milk truck.

What snakes are found on cars?

Windshield vipers.

Where would you take a sick boat?

To the dock.

Who can drive all their customers away and still make money?

Taxi drivers.

What was wrong with the wooden car with wooden wheels?

It wooden go!

What do you get when you put a car and a pet together?

Carpet.

What do you call a motorbike that isn't a Harley Davidson?

A Hardly Davidson.

What's another name for a Rolls Royce Ghost?

A fright on wheels.

Do the buses here run on time?

No, they run on gasoline.

Why do bicycles fall over?

Because they are too tired.

Why couldn't the flower ride its bike to school?

The petals were broken.

What car does an egg drive?

A yokes wagon.

When is a car not a car?

When it turns into a driveway.

What sound does a Witch's car make?

Broom broom!

Why was the car so smelly?

It had too much gas.

Rib-tickling Random Jokes

What do you call a Roman with a cold?

Julius Sneezer!

What did one cannon say to the other?

You're a blast!

What's the capital of Greece?

G.

Why was the Math book sad?

It had a lot of problems.

What colors were television screens in 1824? Black and white or green and orange?

None! There were no TVs in 1824!

How do you scare a snowman?

Show him a hair dryer.

Why can't Elsa from Frozen have a balloon?

Because she will "let it go."

Why did the kid throw a stick of butter out the window?

To see a butter-fly.

What did the triangle say to the circle?

You're pointless!

What did the judge say to the dentist?

Do you swear to pull the tooth, the whole tooth and nothing but the tooth?

What is at the bottom of the sea, trembling?

A nervous wreck.

What do painters do when they get cold?

They put on another coat.

What kind of shoes do spies wear?

Sneakers.

What starts with a P, ends with an E and has over a thousand letters in it?

The post office.

What washes up on very small beaches?

Microwaves.

How do you throw a surprise party for an astronaut?

You have to planet.

What kind of music do mummies listen to?

Wrap music.

Why is it so windy inside a stadium?

There are thousands of fans.

Why is money called dough?

Because you knead it.

What kind of music do balloons hate?

Pop.

What's green and smells like orange paint?

Green paint.

What did one pencil say to the other pencil?

You're looking sharp.

How did the computer catch a cold?

It left its windows open.

What did the janitor say when he jumped out of the closet?

Supplies!

Why was Cinderella dropped from the football team?

She kept running away from the ball.

Which days are the strongest?

Saturday and Sunday, the rest are weekdays.

Which house weighs the least?

A lighthouse.

Why was the broom late?

It over swept.

What do you call a broken can opener?

A can't opener.

Why did the toilet paper roll go down the hill?

To get to the bottom.

Why are circles so smart?

Because they have 360 degrees.

There were two fish in a tank. One said to the other:

"How do you drive and fire this thing?"

Which letters are not in the alphabet?

The ones in the mail.

What do you call a fly without wings?

A walk.

How does a scientist freshen her breath?

With experi-mints!

Which month do soldiers not like?

March.

Why did the cannon have trouble finding work?

It kept getting fired.

What is a sheep's favorite room?

The baaa-throom.

What does the recycling bin like to read?

Litter-ature.

What time do you go to the dentist?

Tooth hurty!

What do you call a witch's garage?

A broom closet!

How did you find school today?

It was right there when I got off the bus.

How do you get straight A's in school?

You use a ruler.

Why do candles go on the tops of cakes?

Because it's hard to light them on the bottom.

How do you know the calendar is popular?

It has so many dates!

What did the blanket say to the bed?

Don't worry, I've got you covered.

Where do televisions go on vacation?

Remote islands.

Doctor, I've broken my arm in two places, what should I do?

Whatever you do, don't go back to those two places!

Why did they bury the battery?

Because it was dead.

Why did the student eat his homework?

Because the teacher said it was a piece of cake.

Why did the computer go to the doctor?

It had a virus.

Why can't you lie to an x-ray technician?

They can see right through you.

Which hand is better to write with?

Neither, it is better to write with a pen.

Which season is best for trampolining?

Springtime.

What has one head, one foot and four legs?

A bed.

Where do snowmen keep their money?

In snowbanks.

Why did the one-armed man cross the road?

To get to the second-hand shop.

What do you call a snowman in July?

Water.

What did zero say to eight?

Nice belt.

Who is Frosty the Snowman's favorite aunt?

Aunt Arctica.

What do you get if you try to multiply 2354 by 4666?

A headache!

How do you look after an upset astronaut?

Give him some space.

How do you get a job in the ocean?

Look in the 'Kelp Wanted' section.

How do you help an astronaut's baby to stop crying?

You rocket.

Why can't you trust stairs?

They are always up to something.

Which flower gives the best kisses?

Tulips.

Who cleans the ocean?

A Mermaid.

Why did Mickey Mouse take a trip into space?

He was looking for Pluto.

What rock group has four members but doesn't make a sound?

Mount Rushmore.

Why couldn't the kids go to the pirate movie?

Because it was rated aaarrrr!

Why did the clock go to the principal's office?

For tocking too much.

Why do witches wear name tags?

To tell which witch is which.

Why is basketball a messy sport?

Because you dribble on the floor.

How do pop stars stay cool?

They get close to their fans.

How do you call someone from jail?

You use a cell phone.

Why did the boy put the radio in the fridge?

He wanted to listen to cool music.

Why do golfers bring spare pants?

In case they get a hole in one.

What do you call a funny mountain?

Hill-arious.

Why haven't you learned the alphabet?

I don't know Y.

Why did the man run around his bed?

He was trying to catch up on his sleep.

Where did the General keep his armies?

Up his sleevies.

Why doesn't Elsa want to get her hair cut?

Because she wants to "Let it grow, let it grow!"

What do you call a donkey with three legs?

A Wonky!

What do you call a snowman in summer?

A puddle.

What does a house wear?

A-ddress.

Why did the chicken join a band?

Because she had the drumsticks.

Where does Santa stay on his vacation?

In a ho-ho-hotel.

Why did the tennis player get a second job as a waiter?

Because he was so good at serving.

What did the drummer call his twin daughters?

Anna one, Anna two!

What do you call a 100-year-old ant?

An ant-ique.

Girl: "What is green and has wheels?"

Boy: "I don't know."

Girl: "Grass! I was just kidding about the wheels."

What do you call bears with no ears?

B.

What do you call a skeleton who won't get out of bed?

Lazy bones!

What gives you the power to walk through a wall?

A door!

Knock Knock Jokes

♦ ♦ ♦

Knock, Knock!

Who's there?

Lettuce

Lettuce who?

Lettuce in!

Knock, Knock!

Who's there?

Boo

Boo who?

Stop crying!

Knock, Knock!

Who's there?

Gopher

Gopher who?

Gopher a walk and I'll tell you when you get back.

Knock, Knock!

Who's there?

Water

Water who?

Water you doing in my house?

Knock, Knock!

Who's there?

Annie

Annie who?

Annie body home?

Knock, Knock!

Who's there?

Nana

Nana who?

Nana your business!

Knock, Knock!

Who's there?

Justin

Justin who?

Justin time for lunch.

Knock, Knock!

Who's there?

Pizza

Pizza who?

Pizza cake would be great please!

Knock, Knock!

Who's there?

I am

I am who?

You don't even know who you are?

Knock, Knock!

Who's there?

Spell

Spell who?

W-H-O

Knock, Knock!

Who's there?

Hatch

Hatch who?

Bless you.

Knock, Knock!

Who's there?

Tank

Thank who?

You're welcome.

Knock, Knock!

Who's there?

Voodoo

Voodoo who?

Voodoo you think you are!

Knock, Knock!

Who's there?

Wire

Wire who?

Wire you not opening the door?

Knock, Knock!

Who's there?

Adore

Adore who?

Adore is between us, open it!

Knock, Knock!

Who's there?

A herd

A herd who?

A herd you were home, so I came over.

Knock, Knock!

Who's there?

Donut

Donut who?

Donut ask me, I just got here.

Knock, Knock!

Who's there?

Ice cream

Ice cream who?

Ice cream if you don't open the door!

Knock, Knock!

Who's there?

Nobel

Nobel who?

Nobel... that's why I knocked!

Knock, Knock!

Who's there?

Doris

Doris who?

Doris locked! That's why I'm knocking.

Knock, Knock!

Who's there?

Police

Police who?

Police can I come in?

Knock, Knock!

Who's there?

Mikey

Mikey who?

Mikey doesn't fit in the keyhole.

Knock, Knock!

Who's there?

Goat

Goat who?

Goat to the door and find out!

Knock, Knock!

Who's there?

Jamaica

Jamaica who?

Jamaica me crazy! Open the door!

Knock, Knock!

Who's there?

Luke

Luke who?

Luke through the peephole and find out!

Knock, Knock!

Who's there?

Scold

Scold who?

Scold out here! Let me in.

Knock, Knock!

Who's there?

Alien

Alien who?

How many aliens do you know?

Knock, Knock!

Who's there?

Stan

Stan who?

Stan back! I'm knocking this door down.

Knock, Knock!

Who's there?

Thermos

Thermos who?

Thermos be a way to get this door open.

Knock, Knock!

Who's there?

Sam

Sam who?

Sam person who has been out here all morning!

Knock, Knock!

Who's there?

Atch

Atch who?

Bless you!

Knock, Knock!

Who's there?

Harry

Harry who?

Harry up and answer the door!

Knock, Knock!

Who's there?

Dishes

Dishes who?

Dishes the police. Open the door!

Knock, Knock!

Who's there?

Figs

Figs who?

Figs the doorbell, I've been knocking forever!

Knock, Knock!

Who's there?

Aida

Aida who?

Aida big lunch today!

Knock, Knock!

Who's there?

Wool

Wool who?

Wool you open up?

Ridiculous Riddles

What animal can you always find at a baseball game?

A bat!

What can you catch, but never throw?

A cold!

Why can't your head be 12 inches long?

Because then it would be a foot!

What is full of eyes but cannot see?

A potato.

A cowboy rides into town on Monday. Two days later, he rides out again on Monday. How is that possible?

His horse was named Monday.

What appears once in a minute, twice in a moment but not once in a thousand years?

The letter M.

What goes up but never comes down?

Your age.

What can jump higher than a building?

Anything that can jump - buildings don't jump at all!

What loses its head in the day but gets it back at night?

A pillow.

What has a thousand eyes but only sees with two of them?

A peacock.

What is red and smells like blue paint?

Red paint.

In a one-story house, the bedrooms are pink, the kitchen is green, and the dining room is red. What color are the stairs?

There are no stairs. It is a one-story house.

What type of lion never roars?

A dandelion.

A dog crossed a river, but it didn't get wet. How was that possible?

The river was frozen.

What start with T, ends with T and has T inside?

A teapot.

What type of room has no doors?

A mushroom.

What has many rings but no fingers?

A telephone.

Give me a drink and I will die. Feed me and I'll become bigger. What am I?

A fire.

If you drop a blue hat into the Red Sea, what does it become?

Wet.

I go around the world but never leave the corner. What am I?

A stamp.

Two men jumped into the swimming pool but only one came out with wet hair. Why?

Because one of them was bald.

How many months in a year have 28 days?

All of them. Every month has at least 28 days!

You buy me to eat, but never eat me. What am I?

A plate.

What comes down but never goes up?

Rain.

What has a bottom at the top?

Legs.

What has hands and face but
cannot hold anything or smile?

A clock.

What type of key can't be used to unlock a door?

A donkey.

What has an eye but cannot see?

A needle.

What gets wet while it's drying?

A towel.

I have a head and tail but no body. What am I?

A coin.

What letter of the alphabet holds the most water?

C.

I can fill a room but take up no space. What am I?

Light.

In times of trouble, what is something you can always count on?

Your fingers.

What kind of cup can't be used to hold water?

A cupcake.

When water comes down, I go up. What am I?

An umbrella.

What has hundreds of needles but cannot sew?

A porcupine.

What word begins with E, ends with E and only has one letter in it?

An envelope.

What is so fragile that it gets broken once you say its name?

Silence.

What is yours but is mostly used by others?

Your name.

What has keys but can't open locks?

A piano.

I am tall when young and short when old. What am I?
A candle.

What can you hold with right hand but not with your left hand?

Your left elbow.

If you look for me, you can't see clearly. If you look through me, you can't see me. What am I?

Spectacles.

I'm the best place in the house to go to escape from zombies. What am I?

The living room.

Why should you never argue with a circle?

Because it is pointless.

Jim's parents have three kids. Two of their names are John and Judy. What is the name of the third child?

Jim.

What gets bigger the more you take away?

A hole.

What makes a loud sound when changing and becomes bigger, but lighter after changing?

Popcorn.

I have four legs, am soft in the middle and hard all around. What am I?

A bed.

I am an odd number. Take away a letter from me and I become even. What am I?

Seven.

If you don't keep me, I will break. What am I?

A promise.

The more there is, the less you see. What am I?

Darkness.

What has a head but no brain?

A head of lettuce.

What has legs but cannot walk?

A chair.

Mrs. Jenkins has five daughters. Each of her daughters has one brother. How many children does Mrs. Jenkins have?

Six. Each of her daughter's brother is the same person.

I wear my shoes while sleeping. What am I?

A horse.

How was it possible for a man to go 10 days without sleeping?

He slept at night.

I can be played or made, cracked or told. What am I?

A joke.

If you imagine you are in an enclosed room with no windows, how do you get out?

Stop imagining.

I get answered without being questioned. What am I?

A doorbell.

What runs but has no legs?

A nose.

What comes up to go and down to stay?

An anchor.

Tongue Twisters

Try saying each tongue twister lots of times in a row. Then try to say them as *fast* as you can.

LEVEL 1 - Getting Knotty

- Proper copper coffee pot.

- Willie's really weary.

- Irish wristwatch.

- Red leather, yellow leather.

- Bad money, mad bunny.

- He threw three balls.

- Freshly fried flying fish.

- Selfish shellfish.

- Fresh French-fried fritters

- Santa's short suit shrunk.

- Pirates' private plank.

- Six slippery snails slid slowly seaward.

- Zebras zig and zebras zag.

Is your tongue in knots yet? If not, try LEVEL 2

- Double bubble gum, bubbles double.

- Clean clams crammed in clean cars.

- Birdie birdie in the sky laid a turdie in my eye. If cows could fly, I'd have a cow pie in my eye.

- A big bug bit the little beetle but the little beetle bit the big bug back.

- How many yaks could a yak pack, pack if a yak pack could pack yaks?

- Gobbling gargoyles gobbled gobbling goblins.

- If a dog chews shoes, whose shoes does he choose?

- Picky people pick Peter Pan Peanut-Butter, 'tis the peanut-butter picky people pick.

- If two witches were watching two watches, which witch would watch which watch.

◆ ◆ ◆

LEVEL 3 - If You Dare!

- Skunk sat on a stump and thunk the stump stunk, but the stump thunk the skunk stunk.

- These sheep shouldn't sleep in a shack; Sheep should sleep in a shed.

- Rory's lawn rake rarely rakes really right.

- Which wristwatches are Swiss wristwatches?

- Lesser leather never weathered wetter weather better.

- To begin to toboggan first buy a toboggan, but don't buy too big a toboggan. Too big a toboggan is too big a toboggan to buy to begin to toboggan.

- How much ground would a groundhog hog, if a groundhog could hog ground? A groundhog would hog all the ground he could hog if a groundhog could hog ground.

- Peter Piper picked a peck of pickled peppers. A peck of pickled peppers Peter Piper picked. If Peter Piper picked a peck of pickled peppers, where´s the peck of pickled peppers Peter Piper pecked?

About The Author

Cillian Bookless

 Cillian (pronounced Killian, not Sillian - even though he can be very silly!) loves to laugh and share jokes with everyone he knows. Many of these jokes are Cillian's own creations and many are well loved classics that have been picked using the patented *Giggle Till You Jiggle* test. This very scientific method has ensured only the funniest and silliest jokes, riddles and tongue twisters are included.

Now get silly, get giggly and get JIGGLY!

Made in the USA
Middletown, DE
16 December 2024

67365516R00066